TREES

Walter Rytz

explains
series

A BOOK IN THE Haynes EXPLAINS SERIES

TREES is published
by
The Haynes Publishing Group of Sparkford, Yeovil, Somerset, BA22 7JJ, England
First published in German under the title
UNSERE BAUME
by
Hallwag AG of Bern, Switzerland

© English language edition, The Haynes Publishing Group 1977
First published July 1977

ISBN 0 85429 509 7

English language translation "Translance" of Manchester
Printed and bound in Great Britain
Cover photograph Siegfried Eigstler
Photographs Eduard Harro Daeniker

CONTENTS

Introduction

What is a tree? A strange question. Everyone knows what a tree is; it is a tall, long-living, woody plant with a trunk and a crown. Of course, but border-line cases are difficult to classify. When is a plant a shrub, and when is it a tree? Are hazel trees and alders shrubs or trees and does one talk about a tree when the whole stem remains within the ground and only two small leaves project above the surface, as in the case of the mountain willow? These are, of course, special examples. Generally speaking we all know what a tree is and if in doubt, we will allow it to be called a tree.

Hence it transpires that individual, usually shrub-like, woody plants are found in books about trees, when they happen to grow up to the height of a tree with a single trunk or if they have close relatives among trees. However, they must be woody plants with a trunk and a crown. Grasses have no place here. Woody plants are perennial and quite permanent. The majority of their cells, except those which carry water from the ground into the leaves, have lignum in the cellulose structure of the cell walls. The thick, woody cell walls are characteristics of trees and shrubs.

The botanist is able to recognise the different kinds of wood by their microscopic picture. Every year a tree forms a new ring of woody cells and the alternating patterns of the wide spring wood and the closely spaced, thick walled autumn wood result in the annual growth rings. Some woods block the innermost trunk parts, which are no longer used, with a hard substance and thence form dark heartwood which can be readily distinguished from the light coloured sapwood. Other trees abandon their central trunk parts to their own fate. They will perhaps decay with time, to the great delight of wild animals who wish to reside within their hollows and very often not to the disadvantage of the tree itself. Hollow lime trees and hawthorns will live for many more years.

This, however, is not malicious damage to the tree. Much worse are the large number of small insects which feed on the wood or on the bark tissue of the tree. Such feeders are the larva of the tree wasp, the tree bark boring caterpillar and the large stag beetle larva. If these insects in their turn did not have natural enemies, then this would result in catastrophic damage to the forests. However, they are kept within reasonable boundaries for it is the express intention within nature's healthy housekeeping that ageing, weak trees are eliminated to make room for young plants. Hence nature keeps itself healthy and the forest, as a large living community, is kept in equilibrium: trees will not grow to the sky and pests will not multiply without restriction, because their enemies will keep them in check. Naturally we should wish to recognise this equilibrium and to maintain it by behaving in the forest as we would in a well kept garden.

Imposing sycamore *(Acer pseudoplatanus)*
At 1400 m (4600 ft) above sea level and in a prominent position. Such well developed trees are a symbol of power and they form graceful landmarks. On walking in the countryside one will find pleasure spending some time in the shade of such a proud giant. A deep reaching, very strong root system anchors this tree firmly into the ground even in the most exposed positions

Successive vegetation communities

This is understood to mean the succession of plant communities, starting from unoccupied ground through to continuous plant coverage, which remain constant unless externally influenced. This step by step colonisation follows **certain firm rules,** and it is not a random development. It is dependent obviously on climatic conditions and on the characteristics of the ground. Hence only those plants which will occur in this living space and which are able to thrive there, can be expected.

The first plant colonisers of empty ground are called **pioneers.** They are rapidly growing, highly adaptable plants, which, however, require a great deal of light and space and good nourishment. Such plants are, for example, flowers on the seashore and in rock niches, colonisers of scree slopes, garden weeds and climbers and mosses on walls. We will call them the initial circle. Their successful competitors form the **transition community.** Wherever they find a free place they will settle and displace the original inhabitants, who may be excessively demanding pioneers, and will spread themselves. This produces a continuous plant coverage, for example high altitude shrubby pastures, scrub, reedy water meadows; our meadows are artificially created transition communities.

Finally arriving are the slowly but steadily growing invincible, strong giants, which also compete among each other and which demand ground and soil; the **final community.** These are found as forests in the majority of areas. The ground cover provided by the transition community is tolerated only to a limited extent or it is expected to adapt itself as an organic part of the final community.

The final communities have different appearances depending on the climatic conditions, soil, exposure (slopes facing north or south) and height above sea level.

Stages

Height in metres/(feet) above sea level	Description	Natural vegetation
over 2500 (8000)	Snow zone	Rock and scree plants Lichen, tundra, early meadows
1900–2500 (6000–8000)	Alpine zone	Alpine plant cover
1800–2000 (5800–6250)	Timber line	Stunted trees, alpine and green alder belt
1200–1900 (4000–6000)	Subalpine zone	Norway spruce forests in Central Alpine zone
600–1200 (2000–4000)	Mountain zone	Beeches
200–600 (625–2000)	Hill zone	Oak mixed forests

Even if in this categorisation, trees are discussed separately as individual living beings with their individual characteristics, the community of trees, ie. the forest in its widest sense, is involved because it represents the natural community of plants. Individual trees, no matter how beautiful they may be and no matter how well they enliven the landscape, in the majority of cases, tend to typify the forming of nature by human beings. We can make comparisons between the natural vegetation of the Jura, the Alps and the Northern (Ligurian) Apennines, both on the northern and southern slopes. In doing this the names given for the level zones, as used in the central area, cannot be used fully. For the designation of the vegetation we will make use of their landscape characteristics, terminology, or the tree names of those which will lend special characteristics to the landscape and to the vegetation zone.

In doing this attention is also drawn to the following:

1. The profiles have to be somewhat simplified; this means that we are restricted to the main types, to avoid confusion. Special influences, such as bodies of water, lakes, rivers, moorlands, or especially the effects of moist sea winds, the Fohn, and the cold and dry north winds will also naturally influence the vegetation; however, they cannot be considered in detail here.

2. Also, unfortunately, the undergrowth, small shrubs and herbs could not be included either, even though they should be included for the completeness of the given forest and woodland picture. For example, it is important to mention the heather in the oak-birch woods of the southern slopes of the Alps.

3. On the timber line, mainly on the northern slopes of the Alps, there extends a bush belt consisting of green alder and of Alpine rhododendrons. In this case the rusty leaved Alpine rhododendron is involved.

4. The snow zone, as the highest vegetation region, is not continuously covered with snow, as would be expected from its name. Vegetation cover would not then be possible at all. We make a distinction between the snow zone and the Alpine zone by considering that where the ground remains free from snow for less than three continuous months, it will no longer possess a continuous cover of vegetation and that there will exist only pioneers, pioneer meadows and the covering vegetation of small plants.

Cross section through Europe with
the more important natural
vegetation zones (level zones) on
the profile line, as drawn on the
adjacent map of Europe

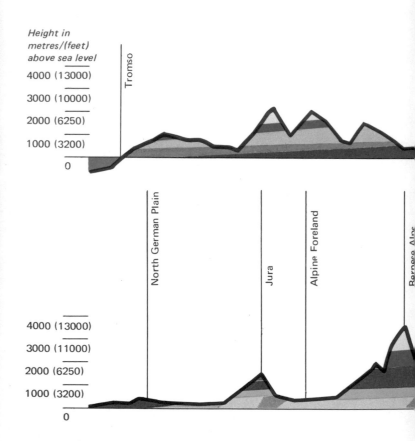

*Height in
metres/(feet)
above sea level*

4000 (13000)

3000 (10000)

2000 (6250)

1000 (3200)

0

Tromso

North German Plain

Jura

Alpine Foreland

Bernese Alps

4000 (13000)

3000 (11000)

2000 (6250)

1000 (3200)

0

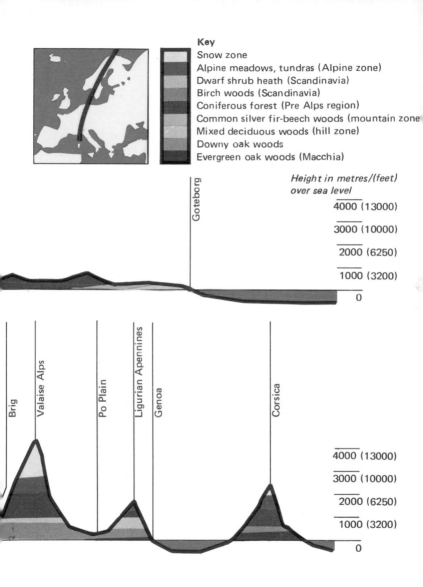

Key

Snow zone
Alpine meadows, tundras (Alpine zone)
Dwarf shrub heath (Scandinavia)
Birch woods (Scandinavia)
Coniferous forest (Pre Alps region)
Common silver fir-beech woods (mountain zone)
Mixed deciduous woods (hill zone)
Downy oak woods
Evergreen oak woods (Macchia)

Goteborg

Height in metres/(feet) over sea level

4000 (13000)

3000 (10000)

2000 (6250)

1000 (3200)

0

Brig
Valaise Alps
Po Plain
Ligurian Apennines
Genoa
Corsica

4000 (13000)

3000 (10000)

2000 (6250)

1000 (3200)

0

9

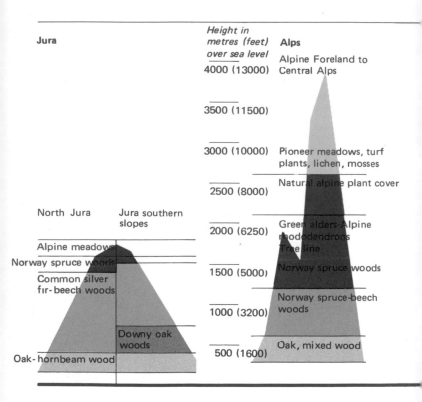

Jura

Height in metres (feet) over sea level

4000 (13000)

3500 (11500)

3000 (10000)

2500 (8000)

2000 (6250)

1500 (5000)

1000 (3200)

500 (1600)

Alps

Alpine Foreland to Central Alps

Pioneer meadows, turf plants, lichen, mosses

Natural alpine plant cover

Green alders-Alpine rhododendrons
Tree line

Norway spruce woods

Norway spruce-beech woods

Oak, mixed wood

North Jura   Jura southern slopes

Alpine meadows

Norway spruce woods

Common silver fir-beech woods

Downy oak woods

Oak-hornbeam wood

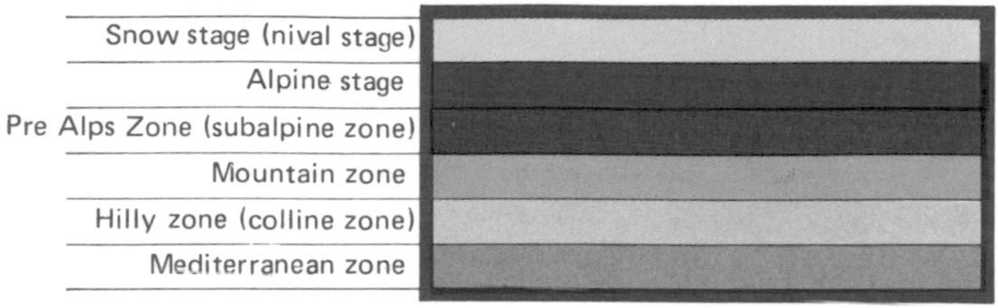

Snow stage (nival stage)		
Alpine stage		
Pre Alps Zone (subalpine zone)		
Mountain zone		
Hilly zone (colline zone)		
Mediterranean zone		

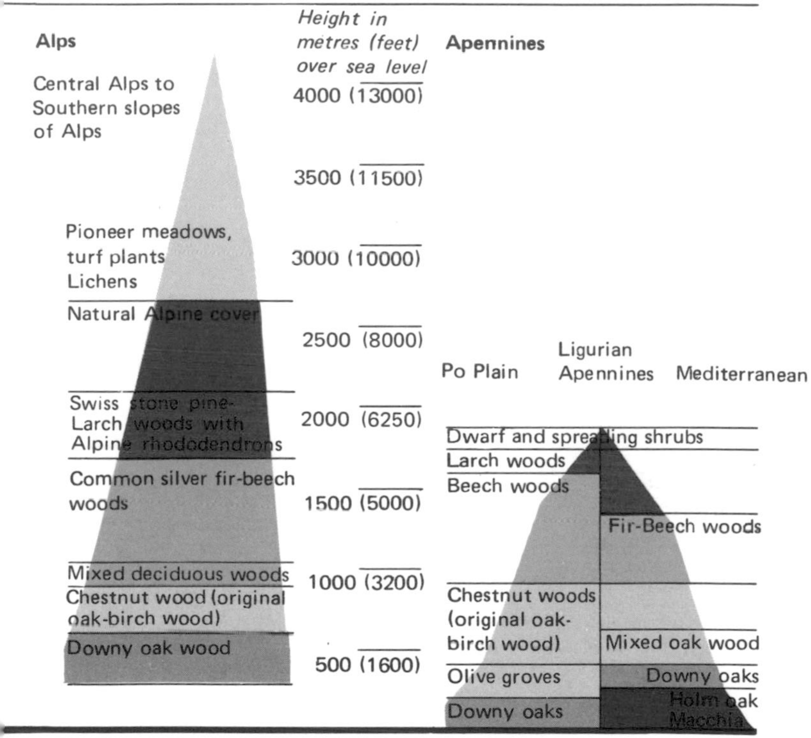

Alps

Central Alps to
Southern slopes
of Alps

*Height in
metres (feet)
over sea level*

Apennines

4000 (13000)

3500 (11500)

Pioneer meadows,
turf plants
Lichens

3000 (10000)

Natural Alpine cover

2500 (8000)

	Ligurian	
Po Plain	Apennines	Mediterranean

Swiss stone pine-
Larch woods with
Alpine rhododendrons

2000 (6250)

Dwarf and spreading shrubs
Larch woods
Beech woods

Common silver fir-beech
woods

1500 (5000)

Fir-Beech woods

Mixed deciduous woods

1000 (3200)

Chestnut wood (original
oak-birch wood)

Chestnut woods
(original oak-
birch wood)

Mixed oak wood

Downy oak wood

500 (1600)

Olive groves

Downy oaks

Downy oaks

Holm oak
Macchia

11

Mountain pine *(Pinus mugo)*
On a steep mountain slope at a height of 1900 m (6250 ft) above sea level.
The prostrate dwarf shrubs and plants in the foreground indicate considerable snow pressure, perhaps also avalanches. The branches of some of the
mountain pines are stripped of needles. Some branches have suffered in the
competition for this position at the tree line boundary; however, the part
which is still living, maintains its claim for this position, until young small
trees have secured their position under its protection. Behind the almost
dead mountain pine are seen the pinnate leaves of the mountain ash

The subalpine Norway Spruce forest *(Picea abies)*
A characteristic feature for the zone between 1200 and 1900 m
(4800—6250 ft) above sea level especially on the northern slopes of the
Alps. The Norway Spruce is at home here and it impresses its
characteristics on the landscape. This tree has a flat root system, as distinct
from the common silver fir which has a tap root and hence requires ground
with deep soil. The Norway Spruce finds less humus at higher mountain
levels, and beneath that, it meets rocky ground. It grips the blocks of rock
with its roots and hence ensures an astonishing grip on the ground

Common beech, silver fir and sycamore woodland
as it appears as a natural community of plants at 1200 m (4000 ft) above
sea level, ie. at the upper boundary of the mountain zone on the northern
slope of the Alps. These highest level of woods of deciduous trees can
become very dense and shady, with the cover and ferns on the ground.
Barely 100 metre (280 ft) higher, beeches no longer live, rather the
Norway Spruce will have become the tree most frequently encountered. In
spite of the sycamore and some grey alders and mountain ash trees it is no
longer a forest of deciduous trees, and it has become a subalpine conifer
forest

Macchia

The well known dense bushy growth of the coastal belt of the Mediterranean countries. Originally forest consisting of evergreen oaks, olive trees and other trees, Macchia is formed as a result of the clearing of the woodland in prehistoric or historical times because the humus dried out and was subsequently washed away by heavy rainfalls. The 'Maquisards' among the plants are extraordinarily resistant and not demanding. These are holm oaks, brooms, rhododendrons and spurge intertwined by thorny creeping plants and trailing heather

Maritime pine
(Pinus pinaster or *maritima)*
A tree of the western
Mediterranean area (Western
coast of Italy as far as Spain,
and Tunis)

Corsican pine
(Pinus nigricans var. Poiretiana)
On the tree boundary on the
Col de Bavella in Corsica, a
tree at higher reaches in the
Mediterranean area

The Northern timber line at 300 m (1800 ft) above sea level
at Skjomen Fjord at Narvik. This is a birch wood. Above the tree boundary
can be seen a circular projecting mountain polished by ice and covered
with sparse Alpine vegetation.
In addition to the stunted birches, this landscape has shrubby willows and
in the moorland it has dwarf birches with small, circular, serrated leaves.
Further south the pine tree appears next to the birches. At the forest
boundary above, the birch woods will become a lichen tundra

A meadow woodland
colonises a river bank and it consists of trees which like gravelly, mineral rich ground and soil but which are also able to withstand the variations in the ground water level. Elders and ash trees, willows and elms, accompanied by a large number of different shrubs, form typical water meadow plants. The oak is only found now and then, the Norway spruce is found more rarely, but beech is never found because it cannot stand the ground water

Norway spruces in the fighting zone
The forest belt boundary is not the final timber line. While the closed
woods and forests will stop at 1900 m (6250 ft), individual trees can occur
at heights up to 2000 m (6500 ft) above sea level. The Norway spruces grip
firmly on the rock at wind sheltered positions in this fighting zone. The
undergrowth is formed by the green alder and by the rust leaved Alpine
rhododendrons. This is the fighting zone on the northern slopes of Alps.
Larches and Arolla pines advance up to 2400 m (7950 ft) above sea level
and stay in these positions in the Central Alpine Massif and on the
Southern slopes

The conifers

These are trees or shrubs with needle shaped leaves, with a few being scaly *(Thuja)*. The majority of them bear cones consisting of broad, woody scales for protecting the seeds and hence they are called cone bearing trees or conifers. Exceptions are formed by the species of junipers and by the common yew which are shrubs with berry-like pseudo fruits. Conifers are evergreen plants, with the exception of the larch, which drops its needles in the autumn and grows new ones in the spring. All conifers have dioecious flowers, ie. pollen carrying flowers (male) and the female, seed carrying flowers.

1. **The common yew** *(Taxus baccata)*. Up to 15 m (50 ft) tall, markedly branched, frequently with a number of trunks with flat needle shaped leaves, upper face glittering and shiny dark green, underside matt and light green. The female common yews produce red pseudo berries every 3 to 4 years. A red, glutinous seed envelope (aril) encloses the seed like a cup. Flowering period: March—April. The common yew tree timber has no resin. The leaves are very poisonous, especially to horses. The male flowers are arranged in small catkins. Occurrence and propagation; individually in shady woods, from Northern Africa to Scandinavia. Demands the least light among all other trees. Sensitive to frost.

2. **The common silver fir** *(Abies alba)*. A tree up to 40 m (130 ft) tall, with whitish-grey smooth bark, which is covered with numerous resin blobs. The needle shaped leaves have a shiny dark green top surface; the underside has two white stripes and these needles are arranged on both sides of the shoot. The cones remain upright on maturing and the scales and seeds will fall one by one. The axis of the cone, known as the spindle (a) will drop off later from the branch. The female flowers produce the cones. The male flowers are arranged in catkins. Occurrence: the common silver fir with its tap roots requires very deep soil and hence it belongs, together with the common beech (Fagus silvatica) in the woods of the upper mountain regions (600—1200 m/1700—3400 ft). Propagation: Pyrenees, Auvergne, Alps, Apennines, Carpathian mountains up to Northern Balkans.

3. **The Norway spruce** *(Picea abies, P. excelsa)*. 25—35 m (80—115 ft) tall tree with red bark. The four sided needles project on all sides from the shoot. This tree flowers profusely every 3—4 years, in May. The ripening cones hang downwards and they release the winged seeds in late autumn, which will germinate partly in the spring; however, they preserve their germinating power for 5—6 years. Natural habitat in the subalpine conifer woods of central and eastern Europe.

4. **Colorado spruce** *(Picea pungens)*. An ornamental spruce, Northern America.

1. **The larch** *(Larix decidua, L. europaea).* A tree 20—30 m (65—100 ft) tall with light green needles growing in clusters. These needles are shed in autumn. Bark greyish brown, fissured, inside red-purple. Flowers April—May, but only every three years or even less frequently. The male catkins are reddish yellow and hanging, but the female cones on the other hand are purple red and erect. Occurrence and propagation: frequently planted in woods and amenity areas. The larch is actually a tree of the higher mountain areas of the Central Alpine massif of Central Europe as far as the Danube. This tree requires the most light in comparison with other trees and hence it is planted in open areas. It prefers low lime, mineral soils.

2. **Common pine** *(Pinus silvestris).* A tree 20—25 m (65—80 ft) tall, with conical crown which becomes domed in older trees. Reddish brown bark which will flake off in older trees. Needles 5 cm (2 in) long, arranged in clusters of two needles. Male flowers clustered in yellow catkins on the upper end of shoots. Female flowers in red cones, at first erect and afterwards pendulous. They require two years for maturing. After that the scales extend and the winged seeds are released. The empty, short cones are released and dropped later. Occurrence and propagation: this tree has few demands where soil, moisture and temperature are concerned. It grows on sand and on dry slopes, where it can anchor itself with its tap root. It resists frost but it requires a great deal of light. This tree spreads from Spain and Northern Africa up to Polar timber line (Lappland).

3. **Mountain pine** *(Pinus P. montana).* This tree is distinguished from Scots pine by prostrate, frequently stunted growth (page 12), a flat root system and dark grey bark. This tree flowers every year in June. Sessile cones, this means that they have no stalks (short stalks in the Scots pine), shiny (pines growing in woods, matt). Main growth area between 1600 and 2300 m (5250—7500 ft) above sea level.

Three subspecies of the mountain pine are to be mentioned: the mountain pine variety *(Pinus P. montana, subspecies arborea)* with straight trunks and asymmetrically positioned cones; the mountain pine subspecies *(Pinus P. montana, subspecies, prostrata),* which is more like a bush or shrub and has stunted growth but which reaches higher regions and forms symmetrical cones: and the variety of the mountain pine growing in moorlands *(Pinus P. montana, subspecies uliginosa)* in moors and bogs. The first subspecies has its home in western and central Europe, the second subspecies has its home in central and eastern Europe down to the Balkans. These trees can be distinguished from each other by the cone scales: in the first subspecies the scale shields are bent backwards in the manner of hooks. The second subspecies has eccentric scale plates, whose upper part is broader than the lower part.
The third subspecies: scale plates symmetrical, upper and lower part equal, spherical bulge in the middle.

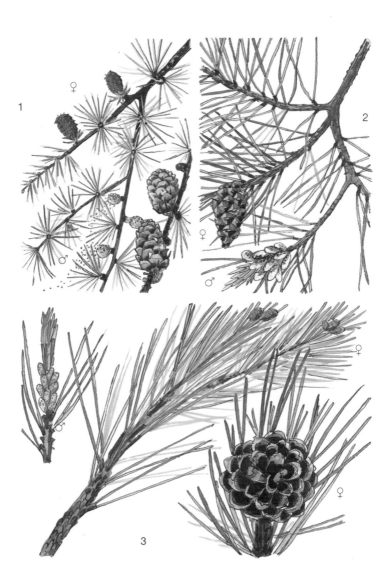

1. **The Corsican pine** *(Pinus nigra = P. nigricans).* On the average a 20 m (65 ft) tall tree, crown becomes domed in older trees, grey-black bark, needles sturdy, pointed, dark green, 8—15 cm (3.0—6 in) long in clusters of two. Cones 5—9 cm (2—3.5 in), hence larger and broader than those of the Scots pine, shiny, outwards spreading. Root system flat, flowers every 2—3 years in May—June. The seeds ripen in the autumn of the second year and they are dropped in the spring of the third year. Very low demanding winter resistant tree, requires a great deal of warmth in summer. This tree occurs in the mountainous areas of Southern Europe, in different varieties, each with their special growing area: the more important ones are the Varietas austriaca ranging from the Eastern Alps as far as Bulgaria and Greece, Crete; the Varietas Poiretiana or the Laricio pine grows in Spain, Corsica, and Southern Italy, and the Varietas Pallasiana grows in Asia Minor and in the Crimea. Female catkins, male catkins with pollen sacks.

2. **The Swiss stone pine or Arolla pine** *(Pinus cembra).* Large, 20 m (65 ft) tall, frequently knotty, thick tree of the higher reaches of mountainous areas, with a number of tops, with grey bark. Needles sturdy, triangular, 4—8 cm (1.5—3 in) long, in clusters of 5 needles. Will become mature to carry flowers only at the age of 60 years! Flowers every 4—8 years, depending on the location. The cones are of the shape and size of a hen's egg, matt brownish grey, loose scaled. Seeds ripen one year after flowering. The almond sized hard scaled, unwinged seeds drop in the spring following the maturing, a desirable food for the nut collecting jay, who is the Alpine cousin of our oak acorn collecting jay. The Swiss stone pine requires a great deal of light, its timber is yellow, interwoven with black branch wood, tough and valuable. Occurrence and propagation: in the central Alpine massif, between 1600 and 2400 m (5250—8000 ft) above sea level, frequently associated with larch. The locations in the Central Alps, the Tatra mountains and in the Carpathians must be regarded as a relic from the glacial period. The main propagation area of the Swiss stone pine is Siberia, ranging from the Ural mountains to Lake Baikal. This tree migrated into Central Europe during the ice age. Its numbers are now greatly reduced. At the Grimsel and at St. Gotthart, where it grew a few centuries ago in great woods, only a few individual trees can now be seen. Hence the reason for the Swiss stone pine reservations (Aletschwald).

3. **The Weymouth pine** *(Pinus strobus).* Large tree, up to 30 m (100 ft) tall, with grey bark, thin, triangular light grey needles, 8—10 cm (3.2—4 in) long, in clusters of 5 needles. 15 cm (6 in) long, loosely scaled resin rich cones. Flowers in May, every 2—3 years. Seeds ripen and drop in the autumn of the year following flowering. This tree comes from North America and was planted in Europe because of its rapid growth and straight trunk. Female cone flowers; male catkins.

Pines in the Mediterranean area

1. **Aleppo pine** *(Pinus halepensis)*. A widely spread conifer of the Mediterranean coastal belt. This tree is 10—15 m (33—50 ft) tall, often has a crooked trunk, reddish grey bark, widely spaced branches and a well spread rounded crown. Needles in clusters of two needles, thin, light green. Cones with short stalks, with high resin content, small. Propagation area: Southern Spain, Southern France, the whole of Central and Southern Italy, Southern Dalmatia and the coasts of Greece, Asia Minor, Tunis, Algeria. Prefers chalky ground.

2. **Maritime pine** *(Pinus pinaster, P. maritima)* A 20—30 m (65—100 ft) tall tree, branched in the manner of firs with long, sturdy needles in clusters of two. This tree has a tap root. Likes granite ground, bark reddish, fissured. Cones large, shiny, pointed. In Southern France this tree supplies resin for making turpentine and colophonium. Propagation: coasts of the Western Mediterranean area: Portugal, Central and Southern Spain, Southern France, West Coast of Italy, Corsica, Sardinia and scattered locations in Alg and Tunisia. In Calabria and in Sicily the maritime pine is absent as also in the Eastern Mediterranean area.

3. **Common pine** *(Pinus pinea)*. A tree 15—20 m (50—65 ft) tall, with mighty, domed crown. An ornamental and useful tree. The pine seeds (in the picture page below on the right) are edible. (Pignoli). The needles are flat and thick, two in a cluster. The bark peels off in plates. This tree demands a great deal of light and hence it thrives only if widely spaced. It grows slowly in comparison with the maritime pine. The lower branches in the shade die out as a result of lack of light, hence the dome shape of the crown. The cones, up to 15 cm (6 in) large, which are round like eggs are situated directly on the branch; they are yellowish brown and shiny. Occurrence: only in the vicinity of the coasts in the whole Northern Mediterranean area up to and including Syria. However, absent in Northern Africa.

On these pines in Southern Europe, mainly on the Aleppo and the Maritime pines, sacks, the size of a man's head, are frequently observed; these are closely woven white nests with greenish brown excrement globules on the underside. These are the nests of the pine tree procession caterpillars *(Thamutopoea pithyocampa)*. These caterpillars have poisonous hairs with sharp hooks, and hence they should not be touched. In the evening they leave their sack shaped woven nests and they walk in a closed train, like a procession, into the upper regions of the tree to eat tree needles. They return to their nest in the morning. Once they are mature, they pupate at the same nest and after incubation there appears a medium sized moth with greyish brown upper and light yellow lower wings.

Conifers as ornamental plants

1. **Cypress** *(Cupressus sempervirens)*. Very slim, frequently 10 or more metres (33 ft) tall, markedly branched tree. The leaves are arranged as triangular scales closely on the branch. The first leaves of the young plant appear as bluish green needles. The cones are balls of diameter 3 cm (1.25 in). The wild form of the cypress has almost horizontal layers of branches. The extremely familiar column-shaped cypress which is cultivated is an important hybrid; it has upright branches close to the trunk. This plant is planted over the whole Mediterranean area or grows wild, and it is planted as a decorative tree in amenity areas and in cemeteries or in rows as protection against wind for plantations. This tree requires mild winter temperatures. Its home is in the area ranging from the Himalayas over the near East to the mountain areas of Persia to Lebanon as far as Crete.

2. **Cedar of Lebanon** *(Cedrus libani)*. A 30 m (100 ft) tall, extensively branched, bluish green conifer. The needles have blue colour when mature; they are stiff, only 3 cm (1.25 in) long, in dense clusters. The cones have barrel shape, approximately 8 cm (3 in) long. The seeds have wings. Planted as an ornamental tree in gardens, which is very useful indeed because this tree has almost completely vanished in its old home, the Lebanon and the Antilebanon mountains, because of its red, very valuable timber. Cedar woods exist still only in Southern Asia Minor.

3. **Atlas cedar** *(Cedrus atlantica)*. This tree is very similar to the Cedar of Lebanon. It has, however, shorter needles, 1.5 cm (.625 in) long. The cones are smaller and more of cylindrical roll shape. Flowers in October. The cones mature in the second year. Considerable cedar woods still exist in Algeria and Morocco, especially in the higher and middle Atlas mountains.

4. **Common yew** *(Thuja occidentalis)*. Medium sized tree, up to 20 m (65 ft) tall, often has a number of trunks, with greyish brown bark and with small, scaly leaves, arranged in four rows which cover the branches. The small brownish green cones have a length of only 1 cm (.4 in). This tree comes from North America and is planted here in gardens, because it is a tree with very small demands; this tree can be shaped as required by suitable trimming (hedges, globular bushes, topiaries).

Deodar *(Cedrus deodara)*. A mountain tree from the North Western Himalayan mountains of Afghanistan and Baluchistan. The main characteristics which are different from those of the other two species of cedar are the overhanging crown, the light green needles. which become up to 5 cm (2 in) long and the large 12 cm (4.75 in) cones which are flattened at the tip.

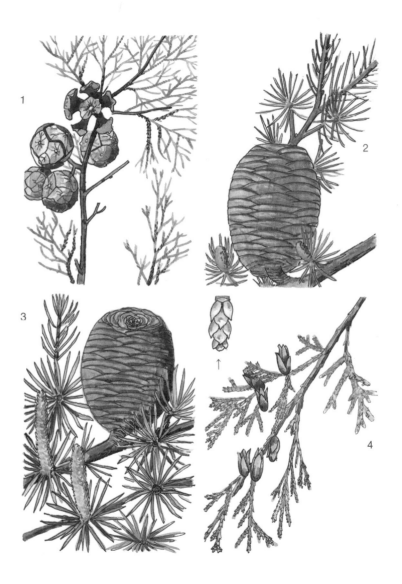

The deciduous trees

These trees belong to the angiospermous flowering plants, and they have covered seeds in their fruits. A number of plant families also contain woody plants in the form of trees. Some of these keep their leaves for a number of years, some of them shed their leaves every autumn, after the valuable processable substances have been withdrawn from these and stored for other purposes (autumn colouring). A separating cork layer is formed on the leaf stalk base which ensures breaking off and seals the breaking point.

Narrow leaved willows

The willows are dioecious trees or shrubs with leaves arranged alternately on opposite sides of the stalk. They never have any thorns. The simple flowers without petals are covered by scales and spaced closely together and hence they form the well known catkins, male   and   female.

1. **Almond willow** *(Salix triandra)*. Tree or shrub, leaves glabrous, shiny, deep green. Long catkins, at first erect, in May, grows on river banks on gravelly sandy ground. Low lying areas.

2. **White willow** *(Salix alba)*. Leaves covered with silky hair on both sides, hence the silvery white appearance, upper sides glabrous in older plants. Leaf edge finely toothed. Flowers April to May. Grows on river banks.

2a. **Lavender willow** *(Salix elaeagnos)*. Shrubby plant, leaves very narrow (4 mm/1.15 in), but up to 10 cm (4 in) long, underside white, edges rolled over. River banks, brook beds, also in Pre-Alps.

3. **Weeping willow** *(Salix babylonica)*. Tree with hanging branches. Large catkins. Cultivated on meadows and in amenity areas. Home: Asia.

4. **Purple osier** *(Salix purpurea)*. Tree or shrub with profusely branched trunk. Young shoots are deep red. Leaves glabrous, their front first part is widest, the edges are finely toothed towards the tip, yellow midrib, bark grey. Flowers March—April. Both pollen sacks of the male flowers are intergrown. This tree likes fresh, damp ground.

5. **Common osier** *(Salix viminalis)*. Tree or shrub with greyish brown bark and long, narrow leaves, leaf edge wavy. Leaf undersides covered with silver white hair. Thick midrib. Flowers March—April. Frequently cultivated beside brooks and near houses. The red globules which are frequently observed on the leaves are caused by a gall mite.

Broad leaved willows

1. **Goat willow** *(Salix caprea)*. Small tree or shrub with light grey broad oval leaves. Leaf underside is covered with grey felty material; the leaf top face is covered only in young leaves, the mature leaves have a glabrous deep green top face. The short leaf tip is frequently curved back. The silky haired female flower catkins appear before the leaves. Flowers March—April. In sunny woodlands and on woodland edges because it requires a great deal of light.

2. **Large leaved willow** *(Salix appendiculata* or *Salix grandifolia)*. In the majority of cases a shrub, occasionally a low tree, very similar to the goat willow. The leaves are, however, still wider, especially in the front third, they have a toothed leaf edge and 1 cm (0.4 in) wide axil leaves. The leaf underside is bluish green with marked spreading hair covered leaf veins. The flower catkins appear together with the leaves in April—June. On rocky slopes.

3.- **Eared willow** *(Salix aurita)*. Shrub up to 1.5 m (5 ft) tall, with thin, reddish brown branches. The leaves have a maximum length of 4 cm (1.6 in); they are rounded and wavy with a patchy felty underside with serrated edges. The axil leaves are ear shaped (hence the name). Flowers April—May. From the plain up to the mountains on moist, lean soils.
Hence a clearly defined shrub was grouped among the trees for reasons of the relationship!

4. **Bay willow** *(Salix pentandra)*. Tree or large shrub with grey bark and pointed oval leaves with shiny green top surface. On the leaf stalk and on the lower part of the leaf edge it has red, globular glands, as small as a lead pencil tip. It flowers in May—June. The male and female catkins are situated on the leaf covered shoots. Like all willow catkins, they are pollinated by insects. The attraction is honey: This is the earliest food in the year for bees! In the majority of cases it is planted as a decorative shrub on wet meadows, in amenity areas and on river banks.

A general remark about the willows is that they are plants of extraordinary vitality. If a willow branch is stuck into the ground a small willow shrub soon grows and thrives. If a willow branch is placed into a container with water, then up to 1 to 2 weeks later it will have produced roots. If possible plant such willow cuttings on river banks and on the banks of ditches. They reinforce the river banks, they will provide shelter for all kinds of useful animal life and they enliven and lend beauty to the landscape.

The poplars

Like the willows these trees are dioecious, ie. they have male and female trees. Their seeds have hairs to assist flying. In the illustrations we see the female catkins with opening fruit capsules. Hair tufts of emerging seeds are visible.

1. **Aspen poplar** *(Populus tremula).* A tree which grows up to 40 m (130 ft) tall, but frequently is only a shrub. The leaves are almost circular and have long stalks, these leaves are always in motion even in the most gentle wind. The edges of the leaves have wavy teeth. The tree bark is grey. Flowers in March—April in downwards hanging, matted hair catkins, the male with red pollen sacks, the female with reddish scarry spots. The timber of the aspen poplar is white and soft, and suitable for making plywood. The tree is not sensitive to cold but it requires a great deal of light, like the larch and birch. This tree spreads from northern Europe (70° latitude), to Northern Africa.

2. **White poplar** *(Populus alba).* Will grow 30—40 m (100—130 ft) tall in favourable areas. Whitish bark, leaves with three to five lobes, underside covered with white felty hairs. Flowers March—April. The young female catkins are thin and yellowish green, the male catkins are thick and reddish brown.

The **grey poplar** with the grey felty leaf underside is probably a hybrid of the aspen poplar and white poplar.

3. **Black poplar** *(Populus nigra).* A frequently met tall tree with grey bark and spreading crown. Leaves are lanceolate, almost triangular, with finely serrated edges. Flowers March—April with slim female catkins and male catkins approximately three times as long. Grows on river banks.

3a. **Lombardy poplar** *(populus nigra var. italica, Populus pyramidalis).* Grows readily to a height of 40 m (130 ft), extraordinarily slim tree, with extended, upright crown, with the appearance of a giant broom. The leaves are similar to those of the black poplar, only less pointed and frequently diamond shaped. This tree comes from the orient and it is planted around country houses (perhaps as a lightning conductor?).

4. **Hybrid black poplar** *(Populus canadensis).* Tall, thick trunked tree with conical crown. Leaves large, triangular, with straight base, shiny deep green. Flowers March—April. This tree comes from North America, it grows rapidly, it demands a great deal of light and it is useful for reafforestation of woods on low lying meadows. Since this tree is not wind resistant, a hybrid of this hybrid black poplar and of the black poplar is now therefore used, as a rule.

1. **Walnut tree** *(Juglans regia).* A 25 m (80 ft) tall tree with pinnate leaves each with 5 to 7 leaflets and grey bark. A large number of male flowers in green, hanging catkins, while the female flowers, small and yellowish, are in clusters of only 2 to 5. This tree flowers in May, usually not every year. Owing to its western Asian origin, the walnut tree is, however, sensitive to frost; it is also very demanding where the soil and light are concerned. This tree produces a very valuable walnut timber. The green fruit shell, like the leaves, is scented and rich in tannic acid. This shell encloses the woody shell which protects the oil rich seeds.

Birches

2. **Silver birch, common birch** *(Betula pendula, Betula verrucosa).* A 15–25 m (50–80 ft) tall tree with white trunk, which, in older trees, has black spots which stand out from the fissured bark. The branches hang downwards and carry triangular leaves with serrated edges. Flowers in March–May; male flowers arranged in catkins, which are formed already in the autumn of the previous year. The female catkins are smaller. Seeds ripen already in July–August. The small fruits have wings. The birch is not a demanding tree where soil is concerned, but it requires a great deal of light. Since this tree is resistant to frost it advances far north up to the Arctic timber line. This was the first tree after the Ice Age in central Europe and it is highly valued as a garden and park tree.

3. **Downy or white birch** *(Betula pubescens).* Small to medium sized tree, bark white like the silver birch. Leaves egg shaped, covered with felty down in young trees. Upright branches. Fruits with small wings. Requires a great deal of light and moist soil. Frequently met on high moorlands (Alpine Foreland, Jura, Vosges mountains). A special subspecies (subspecies tortuosa) covers wide shrub and bushy areas in the extensive moorlands of Northern Scandinavia.

Dwarf birch *(Betula nana).* A small shrub with almost circular small leaves of diameter .5 up to 1 cm (.2–.5 in) with serrated edges. A plant frequently found in Northern latitudes, here, at home, a very rarely encountered relic from the Ice Age; this tree can be found here and there in high lying moorlands.

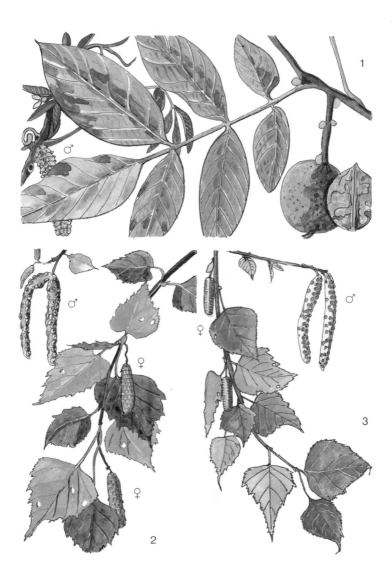

1

♂

♂

♀

♀

2

♂

♀

3

The alders

These trees grow in a kind of symbiosis with a fungus in the soil known as Actinomyces which finds shelter in the roots of this tree. This fungus is capable of chemically joining with the nitrogen from the air and it gives to the alder a contribution of the valuable substances which it forms from nitrogen.

1. **Green alder** *(Alnus viridis)*. Shrub with frequently prostrate trunks, whose dark grey bark has light brown cork projections. The leaves are egg shaped, with alternating deep and shallow serrations on the edges. The underside of the leaf is matt green with projecting ribs, covered with short hair. Flowers in May—June. Very resistant to weather conditions and a tough tree. Occurrence: on wooden slopes and on rocks. Main propagation area above the timber line at 1900 m (6000 ft) above sea level, between the subalpine and alpine regions: the well known alpine rhododendron and green alder belt. The green alder is frequently carried along by wild mountain streams and it then thrives in the lower part of the bed of a stream in the gravel. It is very suitable for reafforestation of steep, slippery slopes of higher mountains. Male flower catkins long and cylindrical, female flower catkins, smaller, egg shaped and formed into clusters. From these appear the cones, which are at first green, then black and finally woody; under their scales lie the little fruits with their thin wings which are scattered into the wind after maturing.

2. **Common alder** *(Alnus glutinosa)*. A tree of height 15—30 m (50—100 ft) with blackish brown bark. Leaves oval with a notch where the tip of the leaf would otherwise be situated. Leaf edges are unevenly toothed. Hairy tufts in leaf vein axils on underside of leaf. Flowers are clustered closely together into catkins, the male and female catkins on the same branches, the male ones long, suspended, the female ones green and sticky, later black and woody. Flowers in March, ripe in autumn. The small seeds and fruits will drop during the following spring. The common alder requires wet ground and a great deal of light. Hence we find this tree near water in low lying areas (lowlands and hilly areas). This tree likes especially the flat moorland peat: hence the alder woods.

3. **Grey alder** *(Alnus incana)*. Medium sized tree or shrub, often with crooked trunk and grey bark. Leaves egg shaped, pointed and doubly toothed on edges, young leaves have grey hair on the underside. Flowers February—March. Habitat: in low lying meadow woods on gravelly ground of the hilly and mountain regions. The timber is dyed orange red by a carotene-like substance.

Common hazel, beech, chestnut

1. **Common hazel** *(Corylus avellana).* This tree usually grows as a shrub, but on occasions also as a tree with a number of trunks, up to 15 m (42 ft) tall with greyish brown bark. Elongated round leaves with pointed tips (the leaf base is heart shaped, different from that of the alder leaf), rough, with serrated edges. The catkins appear in autumn; the flowering time is February—March before the leaves appear. The female flowers are small, more like buds, 2—5 clustered together, recognised by the reddish scars. The fruit, the well known hazel nut, with its cup shaped envelope ripens in September—October. Occurrence; in hedges and open woods over the whole of Europe up to 63° latitude. The red hazel *(variatio atropurpurea)* is a species with a red dye in addition to the chlorophyll.

2. **Beech** *(Fagus silvatica).* A majestic tree with grey, smooth bark and oval, shiny green leaves. A deep purple leaved variety *(var. purpurea)*, the copper beech, also exists. Light red, pear shaped small bodies on the beech leaves, which are frequently observed, are formed by piercing by the beech gall mite and these form shelter and provide nourishment for the larvae of this insect. Another hybrid of the beech is the *var. pendula* with long hanging branches.
The male beech flowers are globular catkins with long stalks, the female flowers have erect heads. They will grow into spiny four valved little beakers with 2—3 beech masts. The flowers appear in May, every 2—3 years. The seedlings the following spring have at first only two thick cotyledons, whose upper side is green and shiny and whose underside is white and felty. The beech is the main tree in the woods of mountain areas. This tree requires deep soil, it does not like ground water, and it produces hard, high quality timber. Propagation: Central and Southern Europe. In the East, in the Black Sea area it is replaced by the oriental beech *(Fagus orientalis).*

3. **Sweet chestnut** *(Castanea sativa).* A 20 m (58 ft) tall tree with spreading, domed crown, with ridged trunk. Leaves up to 20 cm (5 in) long, elongated, tough with pointed edge teeth. The male flowers are in suspended, widely spaced ears. In October the spine covered fruits with 2—3 chestnut nuts *(marroni)* are formed from the female flowers which appear in June. This tree is spread over the whole Mediterranean area and in the Central Europe areas with milder climates.
It is unfortunate that whole chestnut woods are in danger from a parasitic fungus *(Endothia parasitica,* the tree bark tumour), which lives in the timber, for which no treatment is known. Perhaps it is possible to breed chestnut species which are resistant to this pest.

1

2

3

♀ ♂ ♀ ♂ ♀ ♀

The oaks

Majestic trees with interesting shaped leaves and beautiful, hard timber. This tree is demanding where soil and climate are concerned. There are only four species of oak left since the Ice Age north of the Alps; America has more than 80 species! Like the beech and chestnut they belong to the family of trees with fruits enclosed in cups.

1. **Downy oak** *(Quercus pubescens. Q. lanuginosa).* Smaller than the durmast oak and the common oak (20 m/58 ft). The leaves which have long stalks, have deeply scalloped edges, covered with down on the underside. This oak likes warm, dry areas on chalk. This is a Mediterranean plant. When it appears north of the Alps (Southern slopes of the Juras, South East France, Valaise), then it has emigrated during the dry and warm periods about 4000 BC, in the Mesolithic age. Propagation: Northern Mediterranean area, countries around the Danube, Brittany.

The zone in which the downy oak and its associates grow is designated as the downy oak belt (see page 8 etc.). We can study this tree comfortably on the Southern slopes of Ticino and in the upper Italian lakes. This tree is a kind of connecting element between the still drier wasteland belts and the moist, warm deciduous mixed forest belt. On the Mediterranean coast this zone lies directly above the zone of the evergreen oaks (holm oak and the cork oak).

2. **Common oak** *(Quercus robur).* Tall, frequently knotty trunked tree, can grow to several hundred years old. The bark is brown and fissured with a great deal of tannic acid. Leaves have scalloped edges with a short stalk. Frequently produces shoots directly from the trunk. Male flower catkins greenish yellow, female flower catkins, small globular, with long stalks. Flowers every 2—3 years in April—May. Fruits: the acorns in female flowers in their small cups on long stalks, in September—October. Occurrence: mixed deciduous woods of the hilly zone.

3. **Durmast oak** *(Quercus petraea, Q. sessiliflora).* Differs from the common oak by its long stalked leaves and short stalked fruits and by its later flowering time. This tree demands even more warmth than the common oak and it likes raw humus. We find this tree in the Northern European and Atlantic areas in the oak-birch woods together with the aspen poplar and occasional pine trees. The chestnut woods of the Ticino were originally birch-durmast oak woods.

4. **Turkish oak** *(Quercus cerris).* Small tree with leathery, spiked edged leaves, thin thread-shaped yellowish brown auxiliary leaves grow on the base of the main leaf stalk. The acorns are small and dark brown, the shells have long matted hair. Occurs in the dry shrub woods of Southern Europe and the Near East.

Foreign oaks

1. **Red oak** *(Quercus rubra, Q. borealis maxima)*. Large tree with thick trunk, grey bark, and far outwards spreading branches. Leaves with characteristic scalloping, whose serrations will, however, form a sharp tip. Autumn colouring red. The acorns are somewhat larger than those of the common oak, they mature only in the second autumn after flowering. This tree comes from North America. Occasionally planted into our forests.

2. **Holm oak** *(Quercus ilex)*. Evergreen tree of height 10—20 m (34—58 ft). The trunk is relatively slender and grey. The leaves are tough, oval with toothed edges, felty underside. Owing to the sharp tips on the leaf edge it is occasionally confused with the thorny palm tree. The fruits (small acorns) are very small. Spread over the whole Mediterranean area as thick plantations. Very frequently occurring in the Macchias and in the evergreen hardwood deciduous forests.

3. **Cork oak** *(Quercus suber)*. The sister species of the holm oak, but somewhat more knotty, with thicker trunk, but with similar leaves and fruits. The trunk is covered by the well known thick bark, which is peeled off every 7—8 years as cork, pressed and then processed. The decorticated trunks will have a remarkable chocolate brown colouring for a period of time. After that the bark will regrow. The cork oak demands a richer, somewhat moister soil than its less demanding sister. Its main propagation areas are Portugal and Western Spain, South West France, Tunisia, Algeria, Corsica, Sardinia and the Western Coast of Italy and Dalmatia.

4. **Scarlet oak, Kermes oak** *(Quercus coccifera, Q. spinosa)*. The third Mediterranean, evergreen oak. This tree looks more like a bush than the two others. Its leaves are scalloped, with sharp tipped teeth, leathery and somewhat felty on the underside. The short acorn like fruits sit in flat, bristly small cups. The leaves frequently carry red galls, caused by a gall mite. Dyes are made from these galls. The scarlet oak is met in the coastal strips of the whole Mediterranean area, with the exception of Italy. In the Dalmatian countries, mainly in the Northern areas the scarlet oak belongs to the evergreen woods, together with the holm oak, locust bean tree and the three conifers, ie. the pine, the Aleppo pine and the cypress. The undergrowth in this case is formed by the shrubs and grasses of the Macchia.

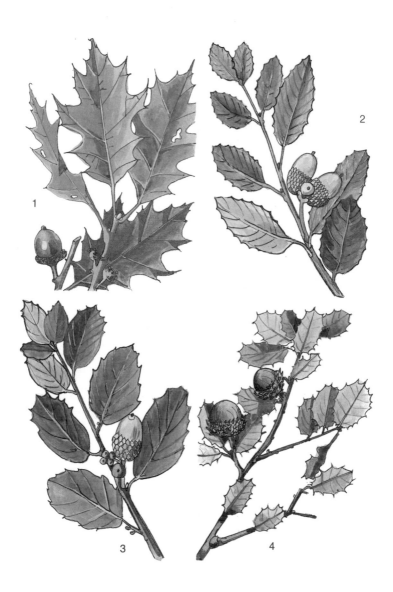

Elms and plane trees

1. **English elm** *(Ulmus campestris).* Large tree with dark brown bark and overhanging crown. The oval leaves, with usually doubly serrated edges, are arranged alternately. Hairy tufts on the underside in the leaf vein axis. The leaf base is markedly asymmetrical. The small dioecious flowers (a) are arranged in dense clusters on the branches. Flowering time March—April. The fruits (b) have broad wings; the small nuts are arranged slightly eccentrically within the wings. The seeds fall as early as June and will germinate in the same year. The tree is a demanding one, and requires mineral rich, well aired soil. Shoots are formed frequently from the trunk. The timber is valuable. This tree thrives well, however, only in warmer areas. This tree belongs to the undergrowth of the downy oak wood.

2. **Wych elm** *(Ulmus scabra, U. montana).* An imposing tree, 40 m (130 ft) tall and higher, with thick trunk and dark brown, slightly longitudinally fissured bark. Leaves large, broadest part at the front, frequently has three tips, covered with rough hair and asymmetrical at the base. The flowers (a) appear before the leaves (March—April) in short stalked clusters. Fruits (b) have wings. The small nuts are arranged in the centre of the wings. The wych elm is less demanding than the English elm and hence it is met more frequently in hilly and mountainous areas than the English elm; in mixed deciduous tree forests, especially in the water meadows on river banks. Planted in streets. However, a parasitic fungus *(Ceratostomella ulmi)* threatens these beautiful trees. This parasite is spread by the elm bark beetle and it kills the tree very often in a very short time (Dutch Elm Disease) if it resides in the trunk.

European White elm *(Ulmus levis, U. effusa).* Very similar to the English elm, however, with long stalked flowers and fruits. The fruit wings have curled edges. A rare, warmth demanding tree with leaves having soft hairs on the underside.

3. **Plane tree** *(Platanus orientalis).* Tree with far overhanging crown and thick trunk whose grey green bark flakes away irregularly. Hence the trunk has a patchy appearance. The leaves are similar to those of the Norway maple, however, the edge of the plane tree leaf continues in the leaf stalk and the main veins have a number of branching points within the leaf. Flowers are arranged in small heads supported by a stalk, the fruits are arranged in globular fruit pods. This is an oriental tree, it likes warmth and it is a popular provider of shade in amenity areas. The London plane *(Platanus acerifolia)* is very similar to this tree and is probably a hybrid between the above mentioned tree and an American species.

Family Rosaceae: 1: Trees producing fruit with pips

1. **Quince** *(Cydonia oblonga, C. maliformis)*. Small tree, approximately 5 m (14 ft) tall, oval leaves, with felty hair on underside. Flowers (in May) are large, white to pink. The fruit is yellow, somewhat felty, dry, and not very tasty when raw, owing to all kinds of substances, which are decomposed on cooking. Cultivated in gardens. Its home is in the Near East.

Leaves and fruits are often infested by a parasitic fungus, in which case they become brown and fall off. If these fallen leaves and other parts are placed on the compost heap the fungus will thrive in the ideal nourishing environment and this enables it to reinfest the young shoots of the quince with its spores during the next spring by means of the rising warm air streams. This pest can be treated with suitable spraying agents. However, the most important remedy would be to collect and burn all diseased leaves and fruit in the autumn!

The quince is related to the splendid flowering quince, **japonica** *(Chaenomeles japonica)* which has fiery red flowers in March and April. The yellow fruits which ripen in October will produce reddish juice on cooking, which will set in the same manner as quince juice (pectin).

2. **Apple tree** *(Pirus malus)*. 5—10 m (14—28 ft) tall tree with well spread branches and fissured bark. The leaves are oval, twice as long as the leaf stalk. Flowers in April—May. The petals are slightly pink and the pollen sacks yellow. There are a large number of cultivated species of the Western Asian-European Apple. Like all highly bred plants, these are exposed to a large number of pests.

A small butterfly, for example, lays its eggs in the apple flower. Its larvae eat the young fruit and are found as an undesirable 'worm' on cutting the apple in two. The fruit is also attacked by parasitic fungi such as the less harmful scab or the virulent monilia fungus *(Sclerotinia)* which causes apples to become brown, soft and covered with concentric rings of white globules and to fall off. Here also the most important precaution is to collect all monilia infested apples and diseased leaves and to burn them all or remove completely.

3. **Pear tree** *(Pirus communis)*. Medium sized tree with outwards spreading branches. Leaves approximately as long as the leaf stalk, shiny green, somewhat tough. Flowers April—May. Petals white, pollen sacks red. The 'false fruit' narrows towards the stalk. This tree also has a large number of cultivated species. The wild form is the thorny European-Western Asian pear.

4. **Medlar** *(Mespilus germanica)*. Small tree, almost a shrub. Grey bark, some thorns on the branches. Leaves elongated, somewhat felty on the underside. White flowers, May—June. Fruit brown with long forward projecting calyx tips, which correspond to the black calyx end in apples and pears. The fruit remains hard and it becomes enjoyable and soft only after the first frost.

Family Rosaceae 2: Service trees

1. **Wild service tree** *(Sorbus torminalis)*. Medium sized tree or shrub with grey bark. Leaves large, with pointed lobes, deep green, autumn colouring red. White flowers in May—June in densely pubescent heads. Fruits reddish brown, with yellow spots. Likes sunny open woods.

2. **True service tree** *(Sorbus domestica)*. Medium sized tree with fine fissured bark and leaves similar to those of the mountain ash, but larger. Flowers white, May—June, pubescent clusters. Fruits have the form of a small, yellowish-red pear, ripe in September, edible. This tree thrives in low lying areas and it can become well over 100 years old.

3. **The mountain ash** *(Sorbus aucuparia)*. 5—15 m (14—42 ft) tall slender tree with smooth, grey bark and pinnate leaves. The leaflets are lanceolate, with serrated edges and white flowers appear in May and June in dense clusters. Fruits (in September) red. In October the leaves will also become bright red. The timber is tough and flexible. This tree is not a very demanding one except that it requires a great deal of light; hence it thrives only in light woodlands and it spreads as the only deciduous tree up to the tree line together with the Norway Spruce.

4. **Whitebeam** *(Sorbus aria)*. Small tree or shrub with large, oval leaves, with serrated edges, upper side deep green, white felty underside. These leaves become carmine red in autumn. Flowers white, in clusters, in May—June, fruits elongated, yellowish red. Location: rocky wooded slopes, low lying river meadows.
A transverse section of the trunk reveals wide, yellow sapwood; this part of the trunk conducts the rising stream of sap. The dark brown heartwood which fills the central part of the trunk is filled and it is very hard and no longer conducts the sap in the tree trunk.

The Arran service tree, Bastard service tree *(Sorbus hybrida)* is the name given to the occasionally appearing mixed species between the mountain ash and the whitebeam. The leaves are pinnate at the bottom, lobed in the middle and towards the tip they are only serrated, their underside is slightly greyish and felty. Also other combinations have been observed.

Mougeot service tree *(Sorbus Mougeotii)* is classified as a species; however, it has perhaps been bred by hybridisation. Its leaves are markedly divided and each division has small edge teeth. Met occasionally here and there at edges of woods.

Family Rosaceae 3: Fruit trees with fruit with stone

1. **Peach tree** *(Prunus persica)*. Small tree, frequently grown as a flat trained tree, with lanceolate leaves whose edges are markedly serrated. Large flowers in March—April with light red petals. The peach fruits have a velvety skin, greenish red or yellowish red, depending on the variety (the latter will ripen later). The 'stone' has a characteristically rough surface; it is hard and large. The tree is apparently of Eastern Asian origin and requires a great deal of warmth, light and nourishment. Its leaves are frequently infested by a parasitic fungus *(Taphrina deformans);* the leaves will wrinkle and the fruit harvest becomes in danger. On some occasions spraying with an infusion of the shave-grass is useful.

2. **Apricot tree** *(Prunus armeniaca)*. Small tree, frequently grown on a trellis, with rounded oval leaves. Flowers in March—April, flowers are large, white, and slightly reddish on the outside. The Apricot fruit is orange red, also with a slightly velvety cover. The 'stone' is almost as smooth as a plum stone. The tree comes from Asia and requires heat and light.

3. **Plum tree** *(Prunus insititia)*. Small tree, young branches covered with hair. Leaves oval covered with hair. Flowers white, arranged in pairs, in April—May. The plum fruits are round, colour depending on the variety yellow, red or blue: Reineclaude, Mirabelle, Sugar plum etc. In the majority of cases the flesh of the fruit adheres to the stone. This plant comes from the orient.

4. **Garden plum** *(Prunus domestica)*. Small to medium sized tree (20 m/58 ft) with greyish brown, fissured bark. Leaves oval and pointed, with serrated edge, underside covered with hair. Flowers greenish white, in May. Fruit elongated, deep blue, with bright blue spots. The 'stone' is flat and sharp edged with pointed ends; this stone is readily separated from the fruit flesh in ripe fruits. This tree also has a number of bred varieties and it also comes originally from the East.

The seeds of all these fruits with a stone contain a substance known as amygdalinum. This substance tastes of bitter almonds: they are, of course, closely related to the almond. This amygdalinum is decomposed under the effect of a fermenting yeast in the seed into sugar, benzaldehyde and prussic acid. This very poisonous acid, known also as hydrocyanic acid, is, of course, generated only in very small quantities; however quantities of the fruit stone kernels should not be consumed.

Family Rosaceae 4: The cherries

1. **Wild cherry, Gean** *(Prunus avium)*. Medium sized tree with grey bark. Leaves elongated with a pointed tip. Serrated edges. We find at the leaf stalk, as in all trees growing fruit with central stone *(Prunus* species) two globular red glands, which are somewhat smaller than a pin head. Flowering time: April—May. Flowers white, fruit globular black or red, depending on the variety, with globular pip. By grafting of good quality scions very tasty varieties with large sized fruit are obtained. The wild form is at home here and in the spring it enlivens the early, attractively green wood edges with its white flowers; in the autumn it enlivens the dark background with its red leaves. The cherry tree requires a great deal of light.

2. **Sour cherry** *(Prunus cerasus)*. It is very similar in its form and size to the wild cherry; the leaves are, however, tougher and both red glands are positioned on the lower edge of the leaf edge and not on the leaf stalk. This tree has white flowers in April and May, and from these it forms deep red, sweet and sour fruits with an oval stone. This tree has also different bred varieties: shade growing Morellos, Griottes. Its home is in the Near East.

3. **Bird cherry** *(Prunus padus)*. A tree of height 10—15 m (28—42 ft), frequently also in shrub form, with dark grey bark. Leaves oval and pointed with sunken veins. Edges finely serrated. Leaf veins are connected to each other near the leaf edge. The leaf stalk has two green glands. White flowers, in overhanging dense clusters. Flowers in May. Fruits round, black bitter sweet but edible, the stone has a rough surface. Occurrence: in light woodlands, in low lying meadow woodlands with damp ground, in hedges, on hillsides and mountainsides.

The 'stone' of these fruits requires a botanical explanation: the fruit has, in fact, three layers. The outside layer is formed by the fruit skin, the middle one by the fruit flesh and the innermost fruit layer is the hard wooden shell of the 'stone'.

This 'stone' is hence not the actual seed, but the innermost fruit layer, whose purpose is to protect the seed. The seed itself has only a brown skin which forms a cover for the seed, which encloses the white seedling with its cotyledons, root and the bud.

Some *Prunus* species are found among the ornamental trees in the garden. The ornamental cherries *(Prunus surrulata* and the Japanese *P. Subhirtella)* with tender pink flowers, the red flowering cherry with brownish red leaves like those of copper beech, a hybrid of the cherry and plum, and others.

Family of the Leguminoseae

The Leguminoseae are given this name because of the butterfly wing like shape of their flowers, although they belong to the pea family. In the majority of cases they have a calyx with 5 sepals from which five petals project outwards. The largest of these which shelters all the rest is called the flag. Under this are situated the two wings which enclose the small boat thus formed. This consists of two petals, which, however, are intergrown at the lower end and which form a kind of keel, to form a complete little boat. This accommodates the 10 stamens which in turn enclose the fruit buds, the latter forming the fruit pod.

1. **Robinia, false acacia** *(Robinia pseudoacacia).* Large tree up to 30 m (84 ft) tall, with dark brown trunk, bark with deep longitudinal fissures. Pinnate leaves, the leaflets are oval, soft. Branches with thorns. Flowers white with brownish red calyx, in profuse, hanging clusters. From these, brown, leathery fruit pods (b) emerge later. This tree originates from North America and it was introduced to Europe by the gardener Robin in the service of the French Kings Henri IV and Louis XIII. This tree requires a great deal of light but otherwise it is not demanding and hence it can be planted wherever desired: in parks and amenity areas: on river banks, on dry dams for anchoring the earth. The robinia grows rapidly and it forms shoots from the trunk even after it has been burnt down.

2. **Wisteria** *(Wisteria sinensis).* A climbing plant whose home is in China. It is planted close to houses owing to its beautiful bluish-purple flower clusters which appear in April and May; here, if it is to some extent exposed to the sun and protected against frost it will grow upwards and will hence decorate summer houses and pergolas. Pinnate, leaves with 7—11 lanceolate leaflets.

3. **Judas tree** *(Cercis siliquastrum).* This magnificent flowering tree in gardens and parks in southern landscapes catches the eye of all observers and hence it must also be mentioned here. Its home is the Near East and the Eastern Mediterranean area. The tree, which is 10—15 m (28—42 ft) tall, is completely covered in early spring with carmine red flower clusters before its leaves appear. The leaves are almost circular, with long stalks and glabrous. The fruits (d) are long, brown pods with a narrow wing on one edge. The name comes from the legend that Judas hanged himself on such a tree.

Maples

1. **Hedge maple, field maple** *(Acer campestre)*. Medium sized tree or large shrub with dark brown trunk, frequently covered with corky ridges. Leaves opposite paired with 3—5 rounded lobes. Flowers (a) yellowish green, regular, each has 4—5 sepals and petals, usually 8 stamens and a double, superior fruit bud. Flowering time: May. The winged double fruits (b) are straight, by which feature this tree differs from other maples. The field maple belongs to the half-shade trees, to the middle zone of the oak and hornbeam woods of warmer areas.

2. **Norway maple** *(Acer platanoides)*. Tree up to 30 m (84 ft) tall, readily recognised by its pointed leaf lobes. The seven main leaf veins all start at the connection point of the leaf stalk in contrast with the arrangement in the sycamore leaf. Yellowish green flowers (a) appear in April, in profuse clusters at the end of stalks. The leaves develop only after the appearance of flowers. The obtuse angled double fruits (b) have wide outspread wings. The main growing areas of the Norway maple are the deciduous woods of the hilly regions with lime rich, slightly damp soils and favourable temperature conditions (Fohn valleys). Frequently planted in parks.

3. **Sycamore** *(Acer pseudoplatanus)*. Up to 30 m (84 ft) tall, with light bark, which flakes in old age in sections. Old trees have knotty trunks and wide outwards spreading crowns. These trees can become hollow because they have no heartwood. Leaves five-lobed, leaf edge toothed. Young shoots are red. Flowers (a) in April—May in yellow greenish, hanging racemes. The double fruits (b) have narrow wings which are arranged at an acute angle to each other. This tree thrives in hilly zones and mountain slopes; however, its home is the subalpine zone, where its habitat reaches 1600 m (5200 ft) above sea level. This tree likes mineral-rich soil, for example river and alluvial areas.

4. **Italian maple** *(Acer opalus)*. Medium sized tree, leaves with 3—5 rounded lobes. Flowers in April. Fruits (b) with lightly spreading wings. Requires dry and warm situation and it belongs to the downy oak woods of South East France, with outwards spreading zones along the southern slope of the Jura mountains, in Valaise and on the Walensee.

The **ash leafed maple** or **box elder** *(Acer negundo)* has pinnate leaves. This tree comes from North America as well as the **Silver maple** *(A. Saccharinum)* which is grown in gardens.

Lime trees, horse chestnut and elderberries

1. **Common lime tree** *(Tilia cordata)*. Tree of height 20—30 m (58—84 ft) with bark which becomes fissured in old age. Heart shaped leaves with long stalks, with shiny green upper surface. Finely serrated leaf edge. On the underside of the leaf orange coloured hair tufts are seen in the leaf vein axils. Yellow, regular flowers, with five petals, appear in June and July. A number of flowers emerge from one stalk which grows in its lower part through a yellowish wing leaf. This leaf will carry the fruit. The aromatic flowers are used to make a popular infusion for a medicinal drink. The common lime tree belongs to the dry oak-hornbeam woods, however, together with the European lime it also belongs to the sunny and rain-rich slopes of the Fohn valleys as a relic from the post glacial warm period.

2. **European lime tree** *(Tilia platyphyllos)*. A majestic tree, grows to height of 40 m (115 ft), forms a rounded crown and can grow very old, even if it becomes hollow due to the absence of heartwood. The leaves are light green, covered on both sides with soft hair, with white clusters of hair in the leaf vein axils on the underside of the leaf. Flowers (a) collected in clusters of 3—5 on the wing leaf, in July, strongly scented. The fruits (b) are 5 sided woody nuts, which are blown over large distances by their wing leaf and which hence spread their greyish brown seeds. The European lime tree decorates many an outstanding position by its presence. However, it is more at home in Southern Europe.

3. **Horse chestnut** *(Aesculus hippocastanum)*. Large tree with overhanging crown and dark brown bark which tends to flake in old age. Leaves hand shaped and divided, usually into seven lobes. Buds (c) light brown, sticky. Flowers (a) white with red spots, large numbers arranged together in upright spikes. Fruit (b), green with soft spines containing 2—3 shiny brown seeds (d). Planted in amenity areas and for bordering of streets. This tree comes from Northern Greece and Northern Asia Minor. Less frequently met is the American, red flowering species.

4. **Alder buckthorn** *(Frangula alnus)*. Small tree (4 m/13 ft) or shrub with light grey bark and widespread branches. The leaves are arranged alternately on the stalk; they are broad and oval, with undivided edges, glabrous. Flowers (a) small, 5 petals, whitish colour, appear in May—June or later. Fruit (b): small, inedible, red, later black fruits with central stone. This tree likes wet ground and is hence met in low lying wet meadows; however, it is found especially in high lying moorlands. This tree has very few demands.

Oil trees and sumach

1. **Ash tree** *(Fraxinus excelsior)*. Tall slim tree with smooth grey bark in its younger years, which will carry almost black bark in old age. Buds black, arranged opposite each other. Leaves pinnate, consisting of 7—13 leaflets. These are pointed and have finely serrated edges. The flowers (a) which are small, pinkish-purple, in tight clusters appear before the leaves, April—May. The flowers have no calyx and petals. Fruits (b) in tight clusters. Fruits are elongated small nuts with tongue shaped wings. This tree is frequently an important part of the mixed deciduous tree woods in the low lying river meadows and in damp woods in the hilly zone, together with the mountain elm, wild cherry, maple, white alder and oaks.

2. **Manna ash tree** *(Fraxinus ornus)*. Small tree, usually less than 10 m (28 ft) tall. It differs from the common ash tree by its smaller pinnate leaves consisting usually of 7 leaflets each with a long stalk, especially the end leaflet. The flowers (a), which appear in April, together with the leaves, have calyx and corolla (each consisting of 4 white small leaves). Indigenous to the Eastern Mediterranean area; however, it grows wild in many other areas or it is planted.

3. **Olive tree** *(Olea europaea)*. A 10—20 m (28—54 ft) tall, outwards spreading, knotty tree with dense crown. Light grey-brown bark. On planting young trees, usually three small plants are planted together which will subsequently intergrow and form the knotty trunk. Leaves are grey green, lanceolate, tough and evergreen. White, multiple flowers (a) appear in May. The fruits (b) are olives, with elongated tip; these fruits contain oil and are highly valued fruits. The olive tree is a typical Mediterranean plant. This tree gives the name to the family of oil yielding trees. These include ash trees, lilacs, liguster, and forsythias.

4. **Wild sumach** *(Rhus typhina)*. A very rapidly growing tree introduced from America, has pinnate leaves and purple-pink flower cones. Fruits red, felty. Valued as an ornamental tree in gardens and amenity areas, it pays to investigate its timber in greater detail given an opportunity. Even if it is only a few years old, this tree has growth rings which are about a centimetre (.4 in) thick, the outside, sap wood-like areas are light yellow, the inner areas consisting of a kind of heartwood are bluish grey.

The leaves change their colour into beautiful red before they drop off in the autumn. In the neighbourhood of a wild sumach are always found seedlings, ie. small trees, which can be readily grown into trees.

Index